Running for Beginners

A Guide for Running for Beginners to get Fit, Lose Weight, and Have Fun.

Colin Adams

Table of Content

Introduction

I want to thank you for buying the book, "Running for Beginners: A guide for running for beginners to get fit, lose weight and have fun".

This book contains proven steps and strategies on how start on your running journey. This book is aimed specifically at beginners but it is also a great reference point for runners who want to start out again after a break.

Everything you need to know about running is in this book. You will find out basics about running and essential information (what is necessary for avoiding injuries, rules of running outdoors, what footwear to purchase).

The book will show you all benefits of running, how to stretch before your runs and how fast you should go. Additionally, you will learn what food you should eat to improve your runs. This book will also teach you how to stay motivated and have fun while you're getting fit at the same time.

Thanks again for buying this book, I hope you enjoy it!

Chapter 1: Why I Wrote This Book?

Running is a wonderful form of exercise. The physical and mental health benefits can be life changing for people who are new to regular exercise.

You have no doubt seen countless joggers in your neighbourhood from very early in the morning to late into the evening and wondered what all what the fuss was all about, why are these people so dedicated?. Running can be highly addictive this is in no small part to the release of endorphins that running gives. The afterglow from a run makes you feel like you are top of the world and I doubt there are many drugs that could compete! A no drug could ever make you as healthy believe me!

I wrote this book after battling for many years with being overweight and suffering from low self esteem. A friend recommended running to me to help me out with the issues I was suffering with and boy am I glad he did. This was over 15 years ago now and I haven't looked back since. Running has helped me overcome so many issues in my life. The buzz I felt after my very first jog,(which was a only a few hundred metres by the way), enabled me to keep going with my running regime A lack of motivation has stopped me from following through with so many different exercises and diets however with running this was never an issue and I put this down solely to the feeling of euphoria that only running can give. As human beings we are designed to walk and run.

So if you have purchased this book then I'd like to welcome you into a wonderful club with millions of members who run every week in order to stay healthy in both body and mind. After following the steps in this book you too will notice how truly life changing running can be.

Thank you and enjoy.

Chapter 2:

Essential Information to Get Started

Running is the favorite activity of millions of people around the world. It is beneficial, plus it costs less than joining the gym.

Before getting started, purchasing running shoes is a must. The best thing to do is to buy running shoes from a store that is equipped with sports gear. The staff are knowledgeable and they can recommend the best shoes for certain people's type of feet.

There are three main types of feet:

•   Flat feet – have fallen arches, therefore they are flexible and prone to overpronation. Pronation occurs when weight is transferred from the heel to the forefoot and the foot rolls inwards.

•   Neutral feet – is the most common type of feet. The runner lands on the heel and rolls forward during the gait cycle until the impact is distributed evenly across the forefoot.

•   High feet – are the opposite from flat feet. When the arches are defined feet end up being rigid, this leads to supination. Supination represents an insufficient inward roll of the feet after landing.

Bearing in mind the different shapes of feet, shoe companies started developing models to accommodate each type of feet. Choosing shoes that are specifically designed for a certain type of feet decreases the chance of getting injured.

Even though the barefoot-inspired, minimalist footwear is fashionable nowadays, it is not recommended to purchase this type of shoe. Before buying minimalist running shoes, it is recommended to wear a "step-down" shoe first.

A "step-down" shoe is minimal, but there is still some slight support to the midsole. It is recommended to purchase these shoes because runners should not go from a firm and stable type of shoe to a minimal shoe type. Wearing minimal shoes requires bones, muscles, tendons and ligaments to strengthen and adjust. Most coaches do not advise wearing this type of footwear every run.

When purchasing, runners should always go for a pair of shoes that felt like they were part of their feet when they were trying them on.

After the new running shoes are bought, runners are supposed to break them in. It is recommended to walk around for a few days wearing new footwear. The feet will get used to new sneakers and the run will be more enjoyable.

When the shoes are bought and the necessary gear for running is ready, it is important to decide when to run. Runners should always strive to run at approximately the same time every day.

Exercise experts are constantly debating about the best time of day for running. Much research has shown that the optimal time to run is when the body temperature is at its highest. For most people the body temperature is at its highest between four pm and five pm. Other research has concluded that runners perform better between four pm and seven pm.

However, morning runs are also useful. Running in the morning keeps the runner motivated. It has been proven that morning exercisers were more consistent with their regimens than people who chose late afternoon or evening runs.

Although people have a natural tendency to run better in the late afternoon or evening, the body can adapt to running in the mornings as well. The runner should choose the best time according to their plans and abilities. Also, they should stick with the schedule in order to get optimal results from their run.

Besides the footwear, there are other essential running items:

• Clothes – should be made of technical fabric. This type of fabric helps runners stay dry and comfortable in cold and wet weather. It is of high importance to avoid cotton. When cotton gets wet, it stays wet, but synthetic wicking material like DryFit, CoolMax, etc. wick the sweat away from the body and keep it warm and dry during winter.

• Running socks – should not be made out of cotton. The best running socks are those that are made out of synthetic material such as polyester or CoolMax.

• Water – because staying hydrated is extremely important. It is recommended to drink four to six ounces of water every twenty minutes during the run.

• ID and money – because every runner has to stay safe while running outside. Therefore, having money in case of emergency is very important.

• Running watch – is meant to time the runs. Even though there are some running watches that measure the runner's heart rate and have a lot of other functions, it is not really necessary. An ordinary watch with start and stop buttons is more than enough for timing runs and comparing progress every day.

• Sun protection – should be applied regularly. Runners spend a significant amount of time outdoors, so the right sun protection is very important. Sunscreen should be waterproof and it should have SPF of at least 15. Also, the ideal sunscreen should offer a broad spectrum of protection (against UVA and UVB rays).

Now, when the gear is purchased and running time is scheduled, you're good to go. Here are some rules every runner should obey while running outdoors:

• Do not take up too much space – when running in a group or by yourself in a busy area, do not force other runners, cyclists or pedestrians off the path.

• Stay to the right – you should stick to your side, and be very careful when you're merging left into a passing lane. Pay attention to cyclists and other runners.

• Follow the usage rules – in case you're running at a location that has strict usage rules, make sure you follow them. If the rules aren't posted, then before you start your run ask someone or just do what they do. Usually, slower runners and walkers use outer lanes.

• No loud music – even though listening to music is a great motivation and helps people focus, you shouldn't turn up the volume to the maximum or should take out one ear bud. You should do so in case there is any obstruction on the path. You should be able to hear what is going on around you.

• Signaling is important – if you have to tie your shoe or decide you will walk for a while, move aside and signal in case there are other runners behind you.

• No littering – when you drink all your water or eat an entire power bar, do not throw anything on the ground.

• Look both ways – especially at intersections, for your own safety.

Chapter 3: Health Benefits of Running

Running is a highly beneficial way to exercise. It represents an essential building block of all other sporting activities. That is why it is no surprise when training programs for athletes whose sports do not involve running, include it as an important part of exercise routine.

Running has many fitness and health benefits.

Contrary to the popular belief, fitness and health are not the same thing. Fitness represents the ability to efficiently expend a lot of energy while health is the state of being free from injury or illness.

Cardiovascular fitness refers to the ability of one's body to absorb oxygen and transfer it through the blood supplies to the muscles. The efficiency of the lungs, heart, and the health of arteries are important factors of cardiovascular fitness. It is especially important for running because the fuel and oxygen required to generate motion are not all stored in the muscles that do the actual work.

Fitness is acquired through the process of physical stress and recovery. For example, when you run, your heart beats faster, muscles work harder and the metabolic system burns more fuel to transfer energy. When you stop running, your body starts recovering and adapting in order to make this process easier in the future.

Every runner should bear in mind that adaptation of the body to running occurs when the runner is recovering, not while running. This is why rest is one of the main components of exercising.

If you want to increase your level of fitness, you must pay attention to recovery.

When it comes to health, running has the following benefits:

- Lower levels of body fat and obesity
- Lower risk of stroke and heart disease
- Stronger bones, reducing the risk of osteoporosis, osteoarthritis and other bone deficiencies
- Reduced risk of getting cancer or diabetes
- Improved immune system
- Stronger muscles, decreased risk of degradation of joints
- Reduced risk of back pain
- Increased coordination and mobility (in older adults)

Running reduces body fat and protects the entire body against chronic diseases related to obesity. Also, running speeds up metabolism which leads to losing weight. Losing weight is one of the primary reasons for why people choose to run.

Inactive people are 20% more likely to have a stroke than people who run regularly. Compared to non-runners, those who run have a 45% lower risk of death from heart-related disease. The interiors of the two ventricles that pump out the blood increase by 20% when you run. This increases the blood supply through your body and benefits several organs. It also reduces bad cholesterol, which in most cases is the main factor of heart diseases and heart attacks.

Runners have stronger bones than inactive people because bones respond to stress by reforming to better handle it. The weight-bearing bones of the legs, pelvis and spine strengthen if the person runs regularly. One of the best ways to prevent osteoporosis is to run regularly. Also, if you already have osteoporosis, running will maintain the bone mass you have. When you run, you do not just build your muscles and endurance, you maintain and build the density and thickness of your bones. According to new studies, recreational running does not increase development of osteoarthritis. It has also been proven that running is beneficial to knee joints.

Researchers have confirmed that running is associated with a reduced risk of colon cancer, breast cancer, endometrial cancer (lining of the uterus), and prostate and lung cancer. As physical activity increases, the risk of diabetes decreases. Running makes skeletal muscles more sensitive to insulin, which leads to glucose being absorbed by cells. Regular running speeds up the clearance of glucose out of the blood. Running also increases blood flow to muscles, which causes higher glucose availability for absorption.

People who run regularly are less prone to cold and flu symptoms during the winter. Regular runs increase immunoglobulin, which is a strong factor in preventing disease. When you run, blood plumps white blood cells through your body faster and raises your internal temperature, which kills viruses and bacteria.

Running decreases the risk of back pain. If you already have back pain, it will help you recover faster. Also, running prevents injuries from returning and reduces the risk of disability from back pain. You should not let fear of feeling the pain stop you from running; as soon as you notice back pain, you should start running slowly and gradually increase the speed. Inactivity leads to loss of flexibility, strength and endurance, which leads to more pain.

Older adults who run regularly lower the risk of falling and fracturing bones due to increased coordination and mobility. Higher bone density also strengthens the entire body.

Other health benefits of running are:

- Regular sleep – running keeps your mind free from distractions that prevent normal sleep.
- Improved brain function – running raises heart rate and increases the flow of oxygen-rich blood throughout your body, including to the brain.
- Helps with depression – running increases the level of endorphins in your body, which elevates your mood.
- Slows aging process – delays aging by maintaining the elasticity of arteries.
- Aids digestion – running speeds up the process of food digestion and helps with the absorption of nutrients from the food you eat.
- Builds endurance – a basic rule of gaining stamina is "work longer, not harder". The more you run the more stamina you build.

Another benefit of running is its positive effect on the lungs. Running increases heart rate which leads to improved lung function. Function of respiratory muscles improves when a person runs regularly.

Running for 30 minutes three times a week can improve:

- Decision-making proficiency
- Memory
- Attention span
- Mental longevity

Regular physical activity can lead to enhanced arousal for women. Additionally, men who run regularly are less likely to have problems with erectile dysfunction than men who are not active.

Running is recognized as a major contributor to good health. Medical professionals consider running one of the most cost-effective ways to improve one's health status.

Chapter 4: Stretching and Warm-Ups

Running can, at times, increase the risk of injury. Starting the run at full speed puts you at risk of pulling muscles, hurting a tendon, joint or bone. This results in you slowing down your speed and, consequently, burning out before completing your work out.

For the above reasons, all exercise experts advise exercisers to warm up prior to going on a run. A good warm up routine allows the muscles, bones and joints to get warm and loosen up. Warming up gradually elevates the heart rate, making it easier to for you to get to the running rhythm you are looking to sustain, allowing you to feel energized enough to run longer, instead of burning out soon and cutting your run short.

Here are some steps that will help you prepare for your run and maximize its benefits:

• Walk – walk at a comfortable pace for three to five minutes. Many people tend to skip on walking and go straight into running, but walking is a perfect low intensity exercise for the transition between the inactive state and into the active state of working out. The movement of walking engages the body's muscles, joints and tendons in motions similar to what these body parts go through during running. Walking also elevates the temperature of the body's muscles and its core, and enhances blood flow into the muscles used during running. Walking is the ideal way to start a run for anybody, but it is especially helpful for those coming back to running after an injury.

• Do Running Strides – Also called pick-ups, running strides are a good warm up activity that takes the body from walking to running. They supply muscles with blood, and they exercise the body's fast twitch muscle fibers. According to expert recommendations, you should do five or six strides, 100 meters each. Strides are done in the following steps:

• Jog at an easy pace for a minimum of two minutes.

• Gradually, start accelerating your pace over the course of 60 to 100 meters. After this, start decelerating.

• After every stride, decelerate into a walk, and walk around while shaking your legs for about 90 minutes.

• After this, walk back in the opposing direction.

• It is not necessary for the strides of your walk to be timed. The distance of every stride is not highly important.

It is important for runners to keep in mind that over striding can lead to injury, so the strides' steps should be kept short and quick, without extending the leg and foot too far in front of the knee.

• Engage in Dynamic Stretches – improve your range of motion using controlled movements of the leg. This will loosen your muscles up, and elevate your heart rate, blood flow and body temperature, all of which will make your run easier and less risky. Dynamic stretches are your best option when compared to static stretches (holding a muscle in fixed position in an elongated position for 30 seconds or more). These static stretches can cause injuries; hence the preference for dynamic stretches. Opt for dynamic stretching routines that target the muscles used in running. Start your stretch slowly, and increase its speed only as the movement gets easier. The first steps should be careful and small, as well as slow, and the motion range should increase gradually as well.

Dynamic stretches routines include the following:

• Skipping – This should be done for 25 to 50 meters, gradually increasing both the range and height of every skip.

• Side step or shuffle – To do this, take steps to the side and go for 10 to 20 meters to the right, then go back the same distance to the left.

• The grapevine – Also called the weave step, the grapevine is done as follows. The right foot is stepped to the right, and the left foot is stepped behind the right one. This should be done for 10 to 20 meters, then repeated in a mirrored manner (to the left)

• Backward jogging – This should be done for a short distance the first time. Fifty meters is a good distance to start with. Begin at a slow speed to avoid tipping and getting injured. Only increase your speed after you get used to the movement, and do so gradually.

• Butt kicks – To do this, walk to the front with a strong backswing allowing your heel touches your glutes. After getting used to this movement, you can try it while you jog. Experts recommend that the movement be repeated 10 times on each side. If this feels easy for you, you can do alternate butt kick with high-knee steps instead. To do this, do five counts of butt kicks and then do five high knees. The butt kicks will work to stretch your quads, while the high-knees steps stretch your glutes. Make sure you only progress to alternate butt kicks only after you have gotten used to doing butt kicks over a long period of time and you feel the need to be more challenged.

• Hacky-Sack – To do this movement, raise you left leg up, while bending your knee so it is pointing out. Without bending forward, tap the inside of the left foot using the right hand. Opt for 10 counts of this movement on each side. This exercise will improve the balance needed for running with minimal risk.

• Toy soldier – To start, maintain straight back and knees, and walk forward raising your legs straight out in front while flexing your toes. To create a more advanced version of this movement, add a skipping motion. This exercise should be repeated 10 times on each side.

Beginners should remember that static stretching is not recommended. Even though it is popular and believed that static stretching prevents injuries, research has proven the opposite. Static stretching can make you strain your muscles, or it can slow you down.

The optimal way to prepare yourself prior to running is to do exercises that focus on getting oxygen to your muscles.
In order to enjoy your run and improve your fitness, do the exercises that are suggested above.

When you finish your run, it is recommended that you do not just stop and stand still. Your body needs to gradually cool down. You can cool down by easing your run and slowing down to a very easy jog for 1 to 2 minutes. Walk at an energetic pace for 1 minute, gradually brining your body back to its resting state. Slow walking speed to the initial, easy effort.

The total duration of the cool down period is 3 to 4 minutes (1-2 minutes of jogging, 1 minute of energetic walking, and 1-2 minutes of slow and easy walking).

Chapter 5: How Far? How Fast?

One of the most common questions that beginners have is "How far I should run?" This question does not have a simple answer. One answer cannot be applied to all runners. The distance of your run depends on your goals and fitness level.

If you've never run before, and did not train in any kind of sport related to running (like football or basketball), you should start gradually. Your very first run should be 0.5 to 3 miles (0.8 kilometers to 4.8 kilometers).

The goal of your first run is not to get fit or to run as fast as possible, the primary aim is to see how your body responds to running. The first run should be comfortable, with an easy pace and you should stop before you get exhausted.

If you played some kind of sport in your past, then you can be more aggressive on your first run. You should aim for 3 to 4 miles (4.8 kilometers to 6.4 kilometers) at a comfortable pace.

Beginning runners should run two to four runs per week for about 20 to 40 minutes (roughly 2 to 4 miles). After a few weeks, you should start adding 5 to 10 minutes to one of your runs in order to have one long run every week. Adding minutes to one run and having long runs is good for beginners as it helps build endurance. Long runs also help increase speed.

When it comes to increasing mileage, those who played football or any other kind of sport can be more aggressive.

It is important to remember that increasing distance of your runs depends on your first run. If you are comfortable completing a certain distance, then you are ready to run that distance as a race; this means that if the distance is relatively easy for you, then you should increase it.

When we are talking about mileage the widely popular "10 percent rule" must not be neglected.

According to the 10 percent rule, you should only increase the weekly mileage in increments of 10%. That means if you are running 30 miles one week, you should run 33 miles the next week.

Researchers and training experts believe there are smarter ways to increase the mileage because the 10 percent rule is too general, and does not apply to all training situations.

The 10 percent rule depends on:

- Being conservative with mileage
- Being aggressive
- Your training cycle
- Involvement of ancillary exercise in training program to prevent injuries

There are three smarter ways to increase mileage:

•   No 10 percent rule for beginners – if you are a beginner, then your main priority is to run consistently and allow your body to get used to running. Two or three days of running 1 to 4 miles should be enough, depending on your fitness level. Do not increase the mileage every week. You should keep the distance consistent for two to three weeks in order to allow your body to adjust. When you are comfortable with your distance, you can run more. If you run three days per week for 2 miles and 3 miles and you are ready for more mileage, it would be wise to add another day of running (2 miles). This is a 25% mileage increase, but it is completely safe. Stick with the new schedule for two to three weeks, and then increase the distance again.

•   No 10% rule if you are coming back from injury – if you take a week off from running, you are not starting from scratch, therefore it is easy to run the mileage you did before the break. However, if that break was longer than two weeks, you have to be cautious when it comes to mileage. Start at a comfortable level, the distance you know you can run relatively easily. Then, every two to three weeks increase the mileage by 10 to 15%.

•   Do not rush to increase the mileage – when you increase the distance of your runs, your body runs more than it has ever run before. If you increase the mileage quickly, your body is stuck in a potential danger zone and can be prone to injuries. Long adjustment is necessary. Do not increase the mileage until you are completely comfortable with running a certain distance.

According to training experts, running consistently is more important than increasing the mileage. Consistency protects your body from injuries and builds endurance.

"How fast should I run?" also belongs to the group of the most common questions that are asked by beginners.

Most daily runs should be done at an easy pace. The best and easiest way to determine the pace is to run slow enough to carry conversation. If you are running in a group, you should be able to speak in complete sentences. If you are running alone, the best way to check if you are running at an easy pace is by trying to sing a song. If you are able to do it without gasping for air, you are doing it right.

Running at a conversational pace or base running has these benefits:

•   Creates a more efficient running style.

•   Helps muscles burn fat more efficiently, receive and process the oxygen better, and deal better with lactic acid.

•   Trains your heart and lungs to be more efficient at absorbing, delivering and utilizing oxygen.

Beginners should try to run at a conversational pace as much as possible. When you build your fitness level and gain more running experience, you can run faster.

It is important not to run every day at the fastest tempo. Running hard every day can lead to injury or physical burnout. Even training experts and fitness coaches do not run every day at the hardest pace. Try to do easy-paced runs at least every other day.

Finally, all beginners should bear in mind that consistency is the most important part of your runs. You should not change your distance or speed if you are not comfortable with the current mileage and pace.

Chapter 6: Foods to Power Your Running

Nutrition is a very important part of running. Food is the main source of fuel to your body muscles. Eating appropriate amounts is what keeps you in a good shape.

The quantity is not the only thing that matters, quality also matters. Runners need both a good quantity and quality foods to provide their bodies with appropriate amount of energy.

All runners should incorporate these foods into their menu:

• Peanut butter with bagel – is extremely good if you are running in the morning. Your last meal (dinner) was several hours ago and your energy level is extremely low. Eating about 250 calorie snack before a morning run gives you enough energy so you can run properly. This snack has carbs, protein and don't take much effort to be digested.

• Berries – are useful due to their high fiber content. They also contain potassium and vitamin C which helps the body to recover.

• Bananas – are an excellent energy booster before running in the afternoon. Bananas are a major source of potassium; it is an essential element in regulating heart beats and blood pressure.

• Broccoli – contains potassium, vitamin C, phytochemicals and fibers which lead to boosting your running performance.

• Lean beef – is a great protein source. Beef is also rich with iron. Iron is an important mineral for all runners. For example, if your body has an iron deficiency it leads to fatigue.

- Low-fat yoghurt – because regular calcium intake is important. Running improves bone density; however runners usually do not get enough calcium. One cup of low-fat yoghurt contains a third of the recommended daily dose of calcium. Also, yoghurt contains protein, which is excellent for building muscles and recovering from tough workouts.

- Wild salmon – is also a good source of protein. Another benefit of eating salmon is the fact that it contains a lot of omega-3. Omega-3 is a good source for maintaining the heart and brain health, and they can counteract inflammation and fend off disease.

If you are a vegetarian and do not eat beef, these foods will have the same effect:

- Beans
- Peas
- Green leafy vegetables
- Iron-fortified cereals

Runners should eat fruits and vegetables, as much as possible; they supply the body with proteins, minerals and carbs. Fruits and vegetables fill the body up with a few calories which help you maintain the weight.

It is recommended to eat five different colors of fruits or vegetables during the day. Each color contains different vitamins and offers unique health benefits.

When you are eating vegetables, keep their skin intact. People tend to neglect the skin of apples, black beans and red potatoes. However, the outer skins of vegetables protect them from UV light and parasites. Those skins contain a wide range of phytochemicals that protect your health. For example, grape skins contain a high level of resveratrol, onion skins consisted of quercetin. Both of the mentioned polyphenols lower the risk of heart disease, colon cancer and prostate cancer, and boost your immune system.

You should also drink milk and eat dairy products that come from animals. Milk, such as from a cow or goat, and other dairy products like kefir, cheese or yoghurt should be a part of every runner's diet.

Dairy products offer:

- Calcium supply which strengthens bones.
- They supply a runner's muscles with a significant amount of protein to speed up recovery.
- Protein found in dairy products improves immunity.
- Milk products contain stearic acid which improves blood-cholesterol levels.
- Regular consumption of dairy foods lowers the risk of heart diseases and regulates blood pressure.
- Runners who include milk products in their diet lose fat faster than those who do not.
- Yoghurt, cultured milk and kefir contain live bacteria which boost immune health and alleviate constipation.

Besides the above mentioned meat, runners should also eat poultry and eggs. All of these foods are rich in protein and protein is needed when you run regularly. Also, meats are a great source of iron and zinc. Regular consumption of meat leads to an increase in red blood cells and improvement of the immune system. These kinds of proteins and minerals are hard to get from non-animal sources.

There are certain foods that runners should avoid. These are:

• White bread – white bread is highly refined and lacks nutrients that whole-grain bread contains.

• Crackers, cookies and cakes – these are filled with calories, added sugar and fat. They do not have the vitamins, nutrients or minerals needed for your health. If you must have a snack, choose products labeled "low-fat", "reduced sodium" or "whole grain".

• Alcohol – even though it is not a food, in order to get optimal results from every run, stay away from alcohol. Alcohol causes slow reactions, decreased performance and increases the risk of injury.

• Caffeine-fortified drinks and energy drinks – because they have dehydrating effects.

When it comes to eating and the timing of eating, the bigger the meal the longer it takes to digest it. It is recommended to eat at least 30 minutes before you start running. Within 20 minutes of finishing your run, have a protein-rich snack to help repair muscle tissue, and carbohydrates to restore your spent energy.

Hydration is important. Regular intake of water has several benefits:

- Fluids regulate the body temperature
- Moves waste from your body
- Ensures the adequate lubrication of joints
- Flushes out the damaged cells that could potentially cause inflammation
- Controls cravings

Another way of staying hydrated is by eating foods and vegetables.

Beginners should pay attention to nutrition in order to get optimal results from their runs. Proper nutrition leads to creating a higher fitness level and speeds up the fat loss process.

If you run to lose weight, you have to bear in mind that you can't lose weight if you do not eat properly. Fitness coaches have a saying "You can't out-train a lousy diet", which means if you do not eat foods rich with minerals, vitamins and other important ingredients, you will not get the desired results.

Runners should not skip meals. You should try to eat at approximately the same time every day.

Make sure to eat properly, and never start running when you are hungry. Food is important because it enables your body to endure the workout, recover from it and become stronger.

Chapter 7: Keeping motivated

In order to run regularly, runners need good motivation. Things you can do to stay motivated include:

• Creating a blog – if you are creative, create a blog where you can write everything about your runs. Make it look like it is your journal which contains updates and notes about each run. You should try to include how far you went, how fast, how you felt after the run and what exercises you did to warm up. Also, it would be great to write about where you were running and what you saw on the way. After some time, when your blog gains a following, you will be excited to go running because you will have new material for your blog later.

• Buying new footwear – just like it was already mentioned in this eBook, proper footwear is important. Promise yourself you will purchase new running shoes if you run regularly.

• Creating a motivating playlist – include songs that make you motivated enough to run. That way you will focus on the songs and will not think about the miles you have left. Research has shown that the psychological effect plays an important role on a runner's fitness. Runners who tend to constantly think about the miles they still have to run get tired faster than runners who do not. Also, always remember the rule of running which applies to listening to music. When you listen to music, always take one ear bud out, and do not turn up the volume to the maximum.

• Choosing a new path – runners usually get bored when they run the same path, day after day. Instead, try choosing a few paths and switch them up from time to time.

• Running in company – having a running partner is beneficial for both parties included. Partners motivate and support each other. Plus, you can have a nice conversation while you are running, which leads to the perception that time went faster.

• Setting a daily goal – these goals can refer to anything you want. They can relate to the style of your run or to your warm-up, it is your choice. When you come up with a certain goal, you automatically want to achieve it.

• Getting a dog – if you are a dog lover or you always wanted to have one but never did, then you should go for it. Having a dog means walking it regularly or having a regular running partner.

• Running for a reason – when you get enough experience, you should sign up to run for a charity. That way, you will be honoring and helping a great and noble cause, while at the same time you have to train and run regularly to finish the race.

• Running solo – applies to people who are stressed out or have a stressful work environment. Running solo helps you clear you mind and you will consider it a great way for psychological relaxation.

• Scheduling – come up with a certain daily schedule. Make sure that the schedule contains all obligations you have to do throughout the day, including your runs. Check off each item on your schedule once you have done it. This will make you want to run in order to check one more thing off of your schedule. You should come up with a new schedule every night before you go to bed, if you wait until you wake up in the morning, you will feel the need to exclude something.

•   Focusing on Zen running – try not to bring your watch from time to time. Instead, focus on your breathing and the sound of your feet hitting the ground as you run. Runners find it soothing and relaxing. Run for the joy of running.

•   Finding a mantra – pick up a short phrase, or come up with your own. Repeat it in your head whenever you feel like you are losing the will to continue. Your own mantra will boost your confidence and desire to continue running.

•   Playing a game – choose one of the road trip games you used to play when you were a child. It is going to be fun for you and your partner. If you're running solo it does not mean you can't play a game. For example, run until you see at least 20 people wearing something red.

•   Buying running magazines – those magazines offer a lot of advice, interviews and suggestions for all runners (both experienced runners and beginners).

•   Changing perspective – do not think about running from the perspective of an inactive person. When you start running, you become active and therefore you should think like it. Do not think about your runs as something you will do IF you have time for it. You should consider your runs an activity you WANT to do.

•   Becoming a role model – when other people see how beneficial running is for you, they will also want to do it. When you inspire other people to do something, you will automatically strive to be even better. If you have children, you will show them how important exercise is. When you lead a nice and healthy life, they will want to do the same.

•   Writing down why you love it – you should make a list of all the reasons why you like to run and keep them in a visible place.

Running can be a fun activity that you will enjoy doing. For example, you can:

• Run with a Frisbee – take a Frisbee with you, go to a park or some other grassy area and then toss it. See how long you can go before letting it touch the ground. That will make you change directions and run in different patterns, which leads to burning more calories and engaging muscles in a completely new way while having fun at the same time.

• Put on a happy face – studies show that the act of smiling (even when you have nothing to smile about) can improve your mood. Also, it has certain health benefits. Smiling is an excellent coping mechanism for stressful situations. Run and smile. You will immediately feel happy and have more fun.

• Be playful – when you feel like it, just skip and hop. This change of pace and playfulness is simultaneously fun and burns calories.

Bottom line, staying motivated and having fun is not as hard as it seems. Once you gain more experience, your fitness level will improve and your body will change. That will be a huge motivation to continue.

Conclusion

Thank you again for buying this book!

I hope this book was able to help you get the information you needed about running for beginners.

The next step is to purchase quality footwear and other essentials. You know what footwear to buy, how to behave while running and how to warm up before every run. You could also find out what foods to eat or not to eat, and the only thing left is to decide when to start your first run.

Finally, if you enjoyed this book, then I'd like to ask you for a favor. Would you be kind enough to leave a review for this book on Amazon? It would be greatly appreciated!

Thank you and good luck!

51674921R00020

Made in the USA
Lexington, KY
01 May 2016